ATHEISTS FOR JESUS

(The title is intended to be mildly jocular, it was originally 'Jesus for Atheists'. Another possibility was 'Introducing Jesus to Christians'.)

By

John Poulton

Contents

Acknowledgements

Thanks to Mark Jones and Mike Bennett for their friendship. Their ideas and questions have informed and challenged me over many years.

Thanks to Nikki Bridgeman for allowing me to use some of her superb artwork for the cover.

Thanks to all the pupils I taught in my thirty years in the classroom. I have so many happy memories and I never regretted becoming a teacher.

I apologise to all those I've irritated and upset when discussing religion in whatever context. I hope I didn't appear too arrogant!

INTRODUCTION

The purpose of this book is to outline the central historical facts about Jesus of Nazareth. Firstly, to suggest how atheists and non-Christians can form a view on 'Jesus the man'. Next, I will explain how this historical Jesus becomes the Christ of Christianity. Finally, I will offer some of my thoughts on how Christians can view the Christ of the gospels in a realistic and fruitful way in the 21st century. Occasionally I will go off at a tangent for the sake of interest. These sections aren't essential to the basic 'flow' of the book, so I will indent those parts and you can happily skip them.

I hope to help Christians and non-Christians find common ground on the subject of Jesus. The ideas in here may also help a Christian answer some questions about the historical person who is at the root of their faith.

This book came about because of a conversation with two old pals of mine on holiday recently in Granada, Spain. We'd had a few drinks and a good laugh. We'd done politics and provided solutions to the country's problems. We'd talked football and sorted our team out. Then, for some reason, our disjointed conversation turned to religion in general and Jesus in particular. This has happened a few times over the years with different people, often in a bar or at a party, though I tend not to bring the subject up myself. I feel uncomfortable discussing religion socially, perhaps because it was my day job for thirty years.

I'm not sure how fruitful our dialogue was that night, and it ground to a dissatisfying halt after fifteen minutes or so. I was left with the feeling that I could have been more helpful. I found, as I had with other people, that they were asking some basic historical questions about Jesus which, initially, I thought they should have known the answers to. Yet, on reflection, I realised that the information they needed is not readily available. Science has charming, photogenic, media pundits like Professor Brian Cox to shine a light on its findings. Sir Richard Attenborough's voice keeps us informed about the natural world. I enjoy their work. But theology has nobody comparable in the national spotlight, and the public is left in the dark. Maybe that's theology's fault, perhaps the media simply isn't interested.

The findings of New Testament, *critical* scholars over the last 100 years have not been widely publicised. This is a shame because so much of the current level of debate is facile and ill informed. 'Critical' here refers to the research methods used. It is the process of analysing scripture using the techniques of modern historical and literary criticism. It challenges scripture rather than simply seeking to interpret it for the believer. Critical theology isn't about what one might call 'blind faith', it asks for evidence to support its conclusions.

I'm writing this to give my buddies' enquiries a full answer, but I'm also writing it for myself. Ideas flutter around over the years, they come in and out of focus. So, I've decided to gather my thoughts in one place and structure them for my own benefit. Partly because writing them down will organise them for me, but also to challenge myself and re-assess my views.

Anyway. The truth, as I hope to demonstrate, is that Jesus was a real person and a historical figure. I think he has rather drowned in misinformation of late. Yet, I believe that people who wish to, should to be able to get sensible answers to sensible questions about him. Unfortunately, in our time the internet, instead of informing people, has tended to drown them in 'fake news'. It has done the same kind of damage to political discussion. For example, I just typed 'Jesus' in Google search. The first item that came up was a story in a national 'newspaper' (Okay, The Daily Express…) which had an article posing the question 'Was Jesus an alien prophet?' That was their religious contribution on Easter Monday. It's pathetic, but all too often that's the level of debate; dumbed down to dumb ass.

Facebook is the trumpet section in this cacophony of stupidity. On the one side are the noisy, well-funded voices of the conservative Fundamentalists, Evangelicals and their ilk. They're usually based in the USA, pro-Jesus, pro-life and pro-guns. They are well versed in the Old and New Testaments but don't know how they were written, preferring to think they were simply dictated by God to the writers. For them Matthew, Mark, Luke and John were secretaries. These people claim to be delivering the 'gospel truth' but it's often served with a hefty side helping of comically bad interpretation. They claim to be traditionalists yet their viewpoint, that all the Bible is historically true, only arose in the late 19th century.

On the other side of the (non) debate is a broad church of atheists, for many of whom denying that Jesus even existed is part of their denial of God. They are partially inspired by their understandable loathing of the conservatives mentioned above. When you read their criticism of religious views, however, they are often ridiculing the religion they were taught at school. They reject Jesus for the same reason they have rejected Father Christmas. They haven't moved on and, ironically, they read the Bible in the same way as the Christian fundamentalists they despise.

There are other voices out there, of course, religion attracts lunatics. There are 'conspiracy theologians', who will make any bizarre claim about Jesus as long it sounds 'radical'. I was debating with a person today who informed me that the Middle East didn't exist, that Jesus was black, with hair like wool and skin like bronze. Like C-3PO wearing a wig. There are probably people out there who believe Jesus was a fish. He hung out at Lake Galilee, his 'friends' were fishermen.

There are so many sources of 'fake news'. The internet allows anyone an equal opportunity to express their opinions, but that doesn't make all opinions equal. As ever, use your common sense when reading, ask for sources, check credentials. If someone claims to be an enlightened member of an elite sect who have a secret knowledge, that only a few chosen initiates... well, you get the picture. Yet, anyone can form a balanced and fair view on Jesus of Nazareth with a little bit of research. This short book will demand no special expertise other than a predisposition to fairness.

To recap, I want to explain how *critical* theology has presented the historical life of Jesus. After that, I want to explain how the Christian view of Jesus came about. Jesus was not a Christian; he was a good Jew who obeyed Jewish Law. Jesus was not the founder of Christianity. Christianity was founded *on* him, not *by* him. Think about it, the core message of Christianity is Jesus' death and resurrection. That message doesn't make any sense until after Jesus has died. Jesus didn't outline the content of Christian teaching, it's not his fault. Don't blame him for Christianity.

When I refer to the "historical life of Jesus" I'm painting with a broad brush. I'm going to outline the main events of his life that a reasonable person could agree with. I'm not going to dwell too much on what Jesus is supposed to have *said*, though. Every line of dialogue in the gospels needs individual analysis, and that would take too long for my purpose here. That's up to you. If you fancy that then, as a rule of thumb, you should try to apply the following criteria. If what Jesus says;

1. Fits his historical, political, and social context of Judea in 30 CE
2. Is about the Kingdom of God
3. Isn't outlandishly unique

Then it's probably authentic. If what he says;

1. Sounds suspiciously Christian
2. Is long winded
3. Contradicts the Law of Moses

Then he probably didn't say it.

The above six rules aren't always easy to apply, but you end up getting a feel for it. We need to bear in mind that Jesus' supposed words were remembered by his listeners and if, as in John's gospel, Jesus starts delivering lengthy monologues, the chances are the section is not trustworthy. Nobody could possibly have remembered such long speeches. I do not claim that Jesus was incapable of originality in his words and ideas, but they must fit his context. For example, Jesus' re-phrasing of 'The Golden Rule' is probably original. He alters the negative Old Testament one;

'don't do bad things to people', to a pro-active version whereby doing good, loving your neighbour, is a duty. Fair enough, I'll give him that one.

I'm not going to burden the text with too much in the way of sources for two reasons. Firstly, if I did, almost every sentence would demand a footnote and reference. Secondly, it would bore me to write it and bore you to read it. I want to present an easy-to-read summary for the lay person, not a turgid textbook. If you want some further reading to check me out, there are some recommendations near the end, and you'll find my views have been drawn from writers like those listed.

My original target when I started writing this was to produce only a dozen sides of A4, because that is all you need to print out the first Gospel, Mark. Given the significance of Mark, it's amazing when you realise how short it is. I know what I want to say here, and there's no chance I can keep it down to twelve sides. After 2000 years, there's a lot that needs to be unsaid.

Cards on the table. Although I don't practise a faith, I am a theist, though I get called a deist. So I believe in a creator god, but I'm sceptical about whether that deity intervenes in the world. I have a degree in Theology, and I was a teacher of Religious Education for thirty years. I haven't been to my local parish Church on any regular basis for a long time now. I disagree with too much of what is said there. Or certainly with how it is presented. Given that, I do miss the congregation of my local Church, as there are plenty of nice people who go there. It's good to have stuff in common and feel part of a community. I do pray from time to time, occasionally using traditional Christian prayers, and I meditate in a non-structured way. I like old cathedrals and churches and when I go in them, I have a moment of silence sat in a pew. And I always light a candle, usually for my Dad.

I'm going to tell the truth as I see it, but that doesn't mean I think I'm right all the time, there's plenty of stuff I don't know for sure. Conclusions about events that took place 2000 years ago can only be tentative ones. Generally, I will be limiting myself to the big picture. The ideas I'll be putting forward here are not original, they're not even new, but for some reason they're not widely known. I'll be as brief as I can without leaving too many gaps.

A SNAPSHOT OF THE HISTORICAL JESUS

The background to Jesus in History (trust me, this is essential); The Players.

The Romans did not conquer Judea (what we call Israel) in the usual way. They were invited in to solve a dispute as the country was politically unstable following the partial disintegration of the monarchy. There was a period of political turmoil following the death of Herod the Great. It's complex! The Romans appointed a governor in Judea and allowed the Jewish people to rule themselves via a council called the Sanhedrin. This council was dominated by a group called **The Sadducees**, the same people who had invited the Romans in. Generally, you would describe the Sadducees as the wealthy elite and from their community (they referred to themselves as a 'tribe') came **The Priests** who ran the religion of Judaism from the Temple. This group, and it really is just one group, the Sadducees and Priests, worked hand in hand with the Romans. They were allies.

Out of respect for Jewish sensibilities, the population was exempt from serving in the Roman military. However, given that the Romans protected their borders and facilitated trade etc, the people were taxed to pay for that security. The key to understanding the tensions in Judea in the 1st century CE comes down to taxation. In other words, money.

The Romans employed a system we could call 'tax farming'. Here's a hypothetical example. Let's say the area of 'Galilee South', is a tax district. Its tax revenue is estimated at one million sesterces. Consequently, the Romans sell the contract for collecting that tax for one million sesterces (or more). Job done. The Roman governor has his tax collected. At this point the contract owner, most likely a wealthy Sadducee, has to collect the tax. So, he recruits a team of tax collectors to go out and gather the money. They will have to collect *more* than one million sesterces for the contract owner to make a profit and for the tax collectors to get paid. They can trawl in as much as they think they can get away with. It's a pyramid scheme, the burden of which falls heaviest on those at the bottom. This set up was lucrative for Rome, for the Sadducees, the Priests, and the tax collectors.

The rich got richer, and the poor got poorer, as money flowed upwards. Inevitably, this situation provoked opposition amongst 'the people'. This opposition divided into several groups, each of which offered their solutions to the problem of growing poverty. However, Judea's tensions, as with Israel today, had a unique character. They understood their land as being God given, the Promised Land, with themselves as the chosen people. Their geographical location and national identity were not an accident of history as mine is, it was part of a divine plan. Politics and religion were not separate. The mere fact of the Roman presence was a cause for anger. The Sadducees and Temple Priests were seen as traitors for collaborating with Rome. It was a blasphemous arrangement which amplified the anger and injustice that people felt. God was their King and Judea his Kingdom. Whatever the method was to be, the outcome at least was clear; the chosen people should be living in *The Kingdom of God,* not some grubby Roman province. The Romans were, after all, non-Jews. The Romans were Gentiles, non-Jews. The word in Hebrew was *goyim,* and it also meant dog. It's not a compliment.

As in any scenario of oppression, one suspects that the largest group would have been those put their heads down, got on with life, and hoped things would get better, but we don't know much about them! Others chose to oppose the regime more directly.

The first group we should mention are **The Pharisees**. They offered a religious response to the growing crisis. Rather than take arms against their rulers and the Romans, they believed that the Kingdom of God was an internal spiritual state. God reigns in your life when you follow His Law. They focused on religious observance and personal holiness. Though they are the bogeymen of the gospels, they were not significant opposition to Jesus in his day. Later, when the gospels were written, this group was running Judea and persecuting some Christians. Consequently, they feature large in the 'Christ' story. They're not important players prior to the destruction of Jerusalem thirty years after Jesus' death. The Pharisees are the target of a lot of New Testament polemic. Possibly Jesus and his followers would have regarded them as cowards, but other than that would have got along fine with them most of the time.

This is one of the big problems with the New Testament versions of Jesus. The gospels reflect the situation they were written in, and it was a *very different* situation in the time of Jesus. It was at least thirty, tempestuous years later. The image of

Jesus they present cannot be taken at face value because they distorted the historical guy. That isn't easy to grasp, perhaps. The gospels are not biographies of Jesus, they are handbooks of Christianity. They don't even try to be history books and so don't directly answer the question which a 21st Century reader wants to ask; 'is this historically true?' Like an archaeologist, we'll have to unearth that truth, scrape off what the early Church added. I'll give an example of this later by analysing one of Jesus' parables. Anyway, back to 'the players'.

Let's have a look at **The Zealots** and **The Sicarii**. We can put these together because they had at least one thing in common in that they were prepared to use violence to further their goal of establishing a tangible Kingdom of God. It meant kicking the Romans out (though there weren't many Romans actually physically present in the country) and dealing with their stooges, the Sadducees and Temple Priests. The Zealots adopted a guerrilla warfare approach, probably mostly aimed at the tax collectors and the guards who protected them. They originated in the north of Judea, in Galilee, where Jesus lived. The Zealot movement played a big role in the Jewish rebellion in the mid-60s, thirty years after Jesus' death. One of Jesus' inner circle of disciples was called Simon the Zealot.

The Sicarii were so called because their weapon of choice was the 'sicae', an easily concealed, curved dagger, which was particularly good for cutting throats. The Sicarius would sneak up on the target in a crowd, whip out the sicae, cut their windpipe and disappear into the throng. One of Jesus' inner circle of disciples was called Judas the Sicarii (Iscariot was not his surname).

Given these two were close associates of Jesus, it is fair to conclude that he and his followers were broadly on the same side as the Zealots and the Sicarii. He had some sympathy, on some level, with the *aims* of both groups, if not with their methods. They all wanted their version of the Kingdom of God to come about. Fortunately, we can link Jesus even more closely to another popular movement of his day.

Let's look briefly at **The Essenes** next. They had monastic set up, lived in community and prepared for the arrival of the Kingdom of God. They were spread across all Judea, but the ruins of a large settlement at Qumran on the shore of the Dead Sea still remain. They are famous today because they decided to hide their sacred texts in some jars in a nearby cave just before the Romans came to finish them off. The Dead Sea Scrolls were discovered in the 1940s. They believed the kingdom was on its way and that they had a mission to prepare themselves and the nation for the event. This group is very important because a key part of their preparation, their purification, in readiness for the coming Kingdom, involved a ritual bathing. This bathing included forgiveness of sins and a re-focusing of one's life to change, turn around, and face a new future. They called this ritual cleansing *baptism*.

They were obviously an influence on a key player in the gospel story, **John the Baptist**. It seems that John toured the region as a wandering prophet, teacher, and general trouble causer. He had a significant number of followers and was highly respected by the population. He preached to people and, if they so chose, he baptised those who wanted to 'sign up' for the imminent Kingdom. At some point in his travels he baptised Jesus, who became an enthusiastic follower of John.

The reason 'The Players' are essential to understanding of Jesus is that they place him in a specific historical context. Far from being an alien prophet, as the Daily Express saw fit to share, he was a man of his time. His views are linked to those of other people of his day. He is understandable in historical, social, political and religious terms like any other figure in history. Okay, it's 2000 years ago and our records may be sketchy, but they aren't non existent. Jesus the man can be known to some extent.

Jesus' childhood.

Did he even have a childhood? Did he actually exist? The first source is the 'Antiquities of the Jews' by Flavius Josephus published around 93 CE. The only reason this text still exists is because the early Christians were keen to preserve it. The reason is clear. Firstly, he refers to the execution of Jesus by Pontius Pilate. The passage has been edited by Christian copyists, but it is clear that Josephus had acknowledged the existence of Jesus. Secondly, Jesus is briefly mentioned a 2nd time when Josephus points out he was the brother of James, about whom he has a lot more to say and his words here are free from later Christian interpolation. Josephus had no interest in Jesus, but he name-checks him. He thought James was the more significant figure. The Roman historian Tacitus writing in around 116 CE also refers to Jesus' execution by Pilate. The Roman governor Pliny the Younger reported on Christian practise around 110 CE, and he assumes the events surrounding Jesus are factual.

These snippets are all one can reasonably expect about a man who barely 'pinged' Roman radar in his lifetime. However, they are evidence of his existence, and no credible historian, atheist or otherwise, denies their essential providence. There are people with vested interests who say 'it's all made up!' and 'he never existed!' The burden of proof is on them, they have to disprove the evidence.

I won't waste any more time on this matter. Yes, Jesus did exist and like anyone else he had a family. His mother was called Mary and let's assume his father was called Joseph. Jesus' dad is a shadowy figure in the gospels and has little role to play, it seems. It doesn't matter. Jesus was born in Nazareth around 3BC, give or take a couple of years. There is one 1 in 365 chance it was on the 25th of December. He had four brothers called James, Joses, Judas and Simon (Mark 6:3) and several sisters, one of whom was probably called Salome. He also had two cousins called Mary and Martha who lived in a village called Bethany just outside of Jerusalem.

You can skip this indented section if you want.

> Perhaps the Christmas story is too famous to ignore, so I'll briefly address it. But it's not essential to understand the Jesus of history because the Nativity is a myth.
>
> One of the advantages of Mark's gospel is that it has less theological accretions than the others. It certainly doesn't have the Christmas stuff. When Mark opens his tale, Jesus is an adult. Jesus' childhood is irrelevant, he's only important for what he does in his preaching career. At the time he was alive, doing his thing, nobody would have known or cared about his unremarkable youth.
>
> However, once Jesus had become the focus of a religion, his followers started developing myths about his childhood. They had to. There were birth myths for the other major figures of the time. Jesus' story would have looked impoverished had he not been furnished with the same. So, the early Christian church went to work. They trawled the Old Testament scriptures, looking for ideas they could incorporate into Jesus' birth narrative. Firstly, they were after ideas that would make Jesus look special. Secondly, and more importantly, they wanted texts that suggested Jesus, and his whole life, were prophesied. Their plan was to show that the events of Jesus' life were no accident.
>
> Of course, by then they knew what had happened, they simply had to find the Old Testament references that made sense of it. They had to demonstrate that Jesus' life was part of a greater, divine plan. Of the four gospels we have in the New Testament, only Luke and Matthew have the Christmas story. Not a lot of people realise that. The question why Mark and John don't bother with the Christmas story isn't asked, but it should be. Frankly, I don't think Mark saw a need for it. John makes up his own tale that has Jesus pre-existing before creation, with God.
>
> The most striking element of the Nativity is the Virgin Birth idea. Matthew based this 'prophecy' on Isaiah chapter 7 verse 14,
>
> "The Lord himself will give you a sign: The virgin will conceive and give birth to a son; he will be called Immanuel "
>
> At least that's what Christian versions of the Bible usually say, but it isn't correct. It's a bad translation of Isaiah, the better texts (like the Revised Standard Version or the Jerusalem Bible Readers Version) will concede this. The original verse in Isaiah said 'young maiden' not 'virgin'.

We know Matthew used a poor Greek translation of Isaiah called 'The Septuagint' which has this error in it along with many others. And, of course, they called him Jesus, not Immanuel. The names don't mean the same either, Jesus means 'God saves', Immanuel means 'God is with us'.

Later Christianity saw Jesus as a new Moses. So, like him, Jesus escapes a slaughter of many innocent children and he is taken to Egypt. The gospel writers used the Old Testament as a source of ideas. Similarly, Jesus is meant to be the Messiah, who was meant to be a descendant of King David, so a 'genealogy' of Jesus' ancestors was invented linking him to David and even Adam. They had no birth records with which to compile such a family tree. Jesus' birth is set in Bethlehem because an Old Testament prophecy said the Messiah would be born there. Had that been the case, Jesus would have been called 'Jesus of Bethlehem'. He never was. He was called Jesus of Nazareth, because that was where he was born.

The Christmas stories are charming, and one can take inspiration from them, but they are myths, not history.

Anything one could claim historically about Jesus' youth is conjecture, but there was one event that must have touched the young man. When he was about ten years old, there was a rebellion in Judea which was brutally put down by the Romans under the leadership of General Quinctilius Varus. The general had 2000 rebels crucified as a punishment. This event hardened opposition to the Romans in the country. If Jesus' father Joseph had been one of those executed, it could explain his peculiar absence from the gospel accounts and Jesus' own politicisation. But this is conjecture however, I have no evidence to back this up.

Mrs. Jesus

Was Jesus married? The question has always been around and more so since Dan Brown's book 'The Da Vinci Code'. I won't indent this section, but if you're not interested, do skip to the next bit. For those who are, let's consider the evidence.

For Jesus being married;
1. There was virtually no tradition of celibacy in 1st century CE Judaism. The quote from Genesis' "be fruitful and multiply", was understood as a divine command and social duty.
2. Mary Magdalene is quite prevalent in the gospel accounts and seems close to Jesus, certainly in Luke. She's described the first witness of the resurrection.

3. After his execution Jesus' body was released to her, it would make sense to give it to his wife.
4. Our gospels are anti Jesus' family, why this is so will be explained later. It's possible that Mary Magdalene was deliberately described as a prostitute to denigrate her because she was his wife. As such, it would have been James' brotherly duty to look after her after Jesus' death, and the gospels are anti-James.

Against Jesus being married;
1. Celibacy was not common, it was very rare, but not unheard of.
2. Mary Magdalene does get a few mentions, but that doesn't make them married, she's just the 'most mentioned female', one woman had to be. Any other interpretation is simply jumping to conclusions.
3. Jesus body was released to Mary Magdalene, but also to Salome his sister and Mary his mother. The last two were close enough family to be the recipients.
4. Maybe Mary Magdalene is described as a prostitute because she was one. Jesus did associate with 'sinners' because forgiveness was a big theme in his mission.

So was Jesus married? Perhaps the gospels gloss over this because in the Judaism of those days women had low status. They could not even be effective disciples because they would not have been allowed to preach in a synagogue as the men did. The truth is that we don't have enough evidence to be certain. However, though the above arguments are equal in number, they are not equal in weight. There are two key points for me. Firstly, it would be quite extraordinary for Jesus, a law-abiding Jew, to disregard the duty to 'be fruitful and multiply'. Secondly, the description of Mary Magdalene as a prostitute looks like an attempt to denigrate her status because, like James, she was family. On balance, I *think* Jesus was married, but I don't know.

John the Baptist

Around the age of thirty Jesus was baptised by John in the river Jordan and became a follower of the Baptist. Jesus baptised people and taught exactly the same message as John;

'Repent and believe, the Kingdom of God is at hand '

The two men were not relatives. The story whereby the pregnant Mary visits pregnant Elizabeth is far-fetched to say the least. The notion of John jumping for joy as a foetus is a device intended to show his inferiority to Jesus. By the time Luke's gospel was written, the early Christian Church was in competition with a similar group who believed John the Baptist was the Messiah. Jesus' subservient relationship as a follower of John was a problem for Christians in the 1st century CE. In Mark, John comically announces that he is not fit to undo Jesus' sandal strap! However, he *must* have been an enthusiastic and committed disciple of the Baptist to get involved in such a practical way. He didn't just get baptized, then sit back waiting for events to take their course. He joined in.

The next significant historical event is the arrest and execution of John by King Herod Antipas (Not the Herod of the Christmas stories, Antipas was one of his sons). John was a popular leader and a thorn in the side of the King. Antipas let John preach and baptise, perhaps fearing a backlash from his followers if he stopped it. However, John was sharply critical of Antipas for marrying his brother's wife, Herodias, and she hated John. He certainly wasn't very complimentary about her and called her a whore.

You can skip this indented section if you want.

> John was slung into prison, but Herod did not execute him straight away. The story goes that the King held a massive banquet and, after some boozy feasting, was particularly enjoying a performance by a dancer named Salome. When she finished, the inebriated Herod stood up and applauded her, promising her anything she wished as a reward for her routine. At that moment Herodias got up, ran onto the floor, and told Salome to ask for the head of John the Baptist.

> We may assume that Herod didn't want to do this but, unfortunately, he had made a very public promise and couldn't back down. A guard was dispatched down to John's cell. He cut off John's head and brought it up to show the party goers. John was shorn of his head and the Baptist movement was shorn of its leader.

It is at this point that Jesus begins his own mission. He takes over from where John left off. Not all the Baptists followers switched allegiance to Jesus, but some did, and Jesus was able to form a core group of disciples. There are various lists of their names, but the magical number '12' is meant to echo the 12 tribes of Israel. The later Christian Church sold itself as the 'New Israel'. Jesus went about the region (probably only at weekends and on the Sabbath) preaching his 'good news' of the Kingdom of God, healing the sick, exorcising evil spirits, and baptising new followers.

I won't go into too much detail about Jesus' missionary activity. He was an itinerant preacher, healer and exorcist, and there were others like him before, during and after his time. His mission, like John's, was to prepare people for the coming

Kingdom. It was about spiritual renewal and personal commitment to the coming struggle. Jesus taught that success was inevitable, as God was on their side.

You can skip this indented section if you want.

Really, do skip this as I am disrupting the narrative flow here. If you're interested, though, I thought I could run a famous parable by you to demonstrate how tricky it can be to understand even Mark's gospel. Jesus drew analogies from nature to make his point quite often. He was often speaking to farmers after all, so he communicated in a medium they would understand. 2000 years ago people did not understand photosynthesis, crop growth was a mystery to them. They planted seeds, they used fertiliser, and they reaped the harvest every year. To ensure the success of the harvest, they prayed and made sacrifices to God. The parable of the sower is a bit trickier than some of 'his' parables because Jesus is actually using a farming analogy to explain why teaching and preaching can be difficult.

"A sower went to sow. 4 As he sowed, some seeds fell on the path, and the birds came and ate them. 5 Other seeds fell on rocky ground, where they had little soil, and immediately they sprang up, since they had no depth of soil, 6 but when the sun rose they were scorched; and because they had no roots they withered away. 7 Other seeds fell on thorns, and the thorns grew up and choked them. 8 Other seeds fell on good soil and brought forth grain, some a hundredfold, some sixty, some thirty. 9 He who has ears, let him hear."	No farmer squanders valuable seeds like this, but we'll ignore that. The message of the parable is simple enough; some people ignore you, some people are enthusiastic but soon forget, some people take your words to heart and you get results. Any classroom teacher sees this every day of their career. The writer of Mark (and, one assumes, his congregation) however is mystified and tries to explain it, so he adds a layer of explanation, putting words into Jesus' mouth.
10 Then the disciples came and asked him, "Why do you speak to them in parables?" 11 And he answered, "To you it has been given to know the secrets of the kingdom of heaven, but it has not been given to them. 12 For to him who has will more be given, and he will have much; but from him who has not, even what he has will be taken away. 13 This is why I speak to them in parables, because seeing they do not see, and hearing they do not hear, nor do they understand. 14 With them is fulfilled the prophecy of	Mark interprets the parable not as a simple, understandable teaching device but as a riddle. He claims Jesus gives out secret messages that are intended to confuse his listener. This absurd, no teacher does that. In Jesus' context of rural Galilee, he was perfectly understood. However, in Mark's context, probably urban Rome, the meaning had become obscure. They probably weren't farmers. The whole Kingdom of God message was specific to a Jewish scenario which Mark's readers

Isaiah which says:
  'You shall indeed hear but never understand,
  and you shall indeed see but never perceive.
¹⁵ For this people's heart has grown dull,
  and their ears are heavy of hearing,
  and their eyes they have closed,
lest they should perceive with their eyes,
  and hear with their ears,
and understand with their heart,
  and turn for me to heal them.'
  ¹⁶ But blessed are your eyes, for they see, and your ears, for they hear. ¹⁷ Honestly, I say to you, many prophets and righteous men longed to see what you see, and did not see it, and to hear what you hear, and did not hear it.
	knew little of.
	
	  Mark ropes in Isaiah to claim that this 'secret teaching' idea was prophesied centuries earlier. He quotes Isaiah out of context making a nonsense of the Old Testament prophet.
	  We see here the crucial shift in emphasis that has taken place between Jesus' day and that of those who wrote the gospels. **The messenger has become the message.** Jesus preached about the Kingdom, but the gospels preach about Jesus. Much of what Jesus said has actually become irrelevant by the time Mark wants to write it down, so he has to change it.

"Hear then the parable of the sower. ¹⁹ When anyone hears the word of the kingdom and does not understand it, the evil one comes and steals away what is sown in his heart; this is what was sown along the path. ²⁰ As for what was sown on rocky ground, this is he who hears the word and immediately receives it with joy; ²¹ yet he has no root in himself, but lasts for a short while, and when troubles or persecution arises on account of the word, immediately he falls away. ²² As for what was sown among thorns, this is he who hears the word, but the cares of the world and the delight in money choke the word, and it proves fruitless. ²³ As for what was sown on good soil, this is he who hears the word and understands it; he bears fruit, and yields, in one case a hundredfold, in another sixty, and in another thirty."	To 'explain' the parable Mark has already turned it into a game of secrets, of hidden, esoteric knowledge. He drops in a new concept, one Jesus never used. Mark talks about the 'word'. The theory behind the 'word' (*Logos* in Greek) is not Christian or Jewish in its origins. To sum up is a Greek philosophical notion whereby the 'Word' is 'reason' or the expression of reason. It goes back over 400 years before Christianity. The early Christians drew upon the concept to express Jesus in concepts accessible to the Greeks they wished to convert, to appeal to them in their terms. It plays a big role in John's gospel where the 'Word was made flesh and dwelt amongst us'. Mark also adds the notion of persecution to his explanation. It's an anachronism, Jesus wasn't persecuted for preaching.

To recap, Jesus was the leader, Rabbi, of his community. He was a healer, teacher, exorcist and baptiser. He also led the group's communal worship significantly at the Seder meal on the eve of the Sabbath every Friday. At this point, I'm going to do some guesswork. There is only one in depth reference to the disciples at worship and that is the Last Supper, but they would have met most

Fridays if they were in the vicinity and able to. I'm going to hazard a guess at the nature of their worship because I think it could explain something very important later.

I think the worship led by Jesus had a *charismatic* quality to it. By this I mean that it was not solely centred on the formal recitation of scripture and traditional prayers. I think it would have been spiritually intense, freely structured, and emotionally charged. It would have felt <u>transcendent</u> compared to mundane daily life. If one looks at Jesus' response to his baptism by John then, clearly, it was a spiritual, religious experience that Jesus had. Jesus provoked similar religious experiences in those he ministered to. That is the very core of his healing. It may have involved the phenomenon known as 'praying in tongues'. This 'holy gibbering' is not attractive to the intellectual perhaps, but it is recorded in The Book of Acts at Pentecost. St Paul had to battle the chaos caused by excessive charismatic worship, specifically 'praying in tongues' in the Church he founded in Corinth. It's a clearly present in the early Church and it's reasonable to assume the practice stretches back to when Jesus was alive. More of this later.

The Last Week

I am trying to give an explanation of how events led to Jesus' death without resorting to supernatural or miraculous devices. It may look like I am 'cherry picking' the details as presented in the gospels and indeed, I am. My rationale is that I will use the details that seem like reasonable occurrences, the events that fit in with what we know of Jesus and his cultural milieu. This is the 'reductionist' approach, which many Christians do not like, as it seems to leave no room for divine intervention. Fair enough, but I want to explain events in such a manner that an atheist could accept as reasonable.

Palm Sunday

It is an undisputed fact that in the last week of Jesus' life he and his followers, friends and family from Capernaum in Galilee, headed south to Jerusalem to celebrate the Passover. Christianity celebrates his arrival there with Palm Sunday. In the gospel version of the story, the cheers of the crowd are directed at Jesus,

'Hosanna, blessings on him who comes in the name of our father, King David.'

I'm sure they did sing this, they still sing it today, but it's not directed at Jesus. He would have been joining in. It's a traditional psalm for the occasion. Jesus was not hailed as a Messiah by the crowd. Why would he be? The Messiah was believed to be a politician, a military leader, and a royal personage. Jesus was none of these things. We assume they had a pleasant time and headed off to their accommodation.

That was in Bethany, about a mile and a half away, down the valley and through the olive groves on the slopes opposite the city. Jesus had relatives there.

We may assume the group headed into the city most days that week. Passover was a massive annual festival, attracting Jewish believers from all over the Mediterranean and the Roman Empire. It is possible that up to half a million people camped outside the city walls. It would have been quite a jamboree, the Woodstock of its day!

It was the biggest feast in the Jewish calendar and a massive money spinner for the city, the Temple, the Priests and the Romans. There was a market in the Gentile Court of the Temple selling animals for slaughter on the altar. If you brought your own beast, the priests would be sure to find a flaw in it and reject as unfit for sacrifice. You would be directed to buy an official one at inflated prices. There were stalls for changing money, there had to be. The second commandment stated, 'You shall have no false gods before me'. Consequently, you couldn't take Roman coins into the Temple because they had the face of Caesar printed on them. Caesar was a pagan god, so Roman denarii were rightly exchanged for Jewish shekels.

The Riot in the Temple

Jesus would not have objected to the money changers or the market stalls because they had to be there. They were only situated in the outer Temple court, the Gentile area, not the Holy of Holies. The most sensible reading of events is that he did give an inflammatory speech which led to a riot. His theme would probably have been a tirade against the unjust taxes and the traitorous collaboration of the Sadducees and Priests with the Romans. Jesus' words found a ready audience and in the ensuing chaos the market was trashed.

It's my contention that this is the event that brings Jesus to the attention of the authorities. His disruption of the market cost them a lot of money in lost taxes and stolen/destroyed goods. I don't think his Kingdom of God preaching message was the issue. He had only worked in a remote area, Galilee, away from the centre of power and authority. He had been preaching for a while and it was the same message as the Essenes and John the Baptist. I don't think the powers of the day saw Jesus as a significant revolutionary threat because he did not have many followers. However, the riot in the Temple hit them where it hurt most, in their pockets.

The Sadducees and Priests wanted revenge, and they wanted to make an example of Jesus, so a warrant was put out for his arrest. A wanted poster if you like, with a reward of thirty pieces of silver for information that would lead to his capture.

Nevertheless, it would have been very difficult to find Jesus. He was most likely an unknown figure in Jerusalem. There were hundreds of thousands of pilgrims all over the city and camped outside its walls. Jesus wasn't even staying there, anyway.

Had he wandered into town perhaps they could have arrested him, but they wouldn't have been so sure what he looked like. There was perhaps a danger that he could incite another riot. Had Jesus gone back to Galilee at this point, and kept his head down, it's possible he would have got away with causing the punch up in the Temple.

The Last Supper, their Passover meal

Part of the 'buzz' of Passover week for the pilgrims was the tradition of eating the Passover meal within the city walls. To accommodate the large numbers, the Priests made a special dispensation that, for one week only, it was acceptable to have the special meal on any night in the city. There would only have been so many suitable rooms one could book. Jesus and his disciples made arrangements to eat on the Thursday rather than the traditional Friday. It was probably less expensive to hire a room for that night too.

As they sat down to eat Jesus must have known that if he could evade capture, he would be safe back in Galilee. But as he looked around the room, he noticed Judas was missing. Maybe Judas left during the meal, it doesn't matter. It is impossible to guess Judas' motives, but we can safely conclude that the relationship between the two was in a bad state. Jesus will have known about the price on his head, when he saw Judas was not there, he will have guessed where he had gone. Judas was going to betray him.

At this moment, and only at this moment, Jesus realised that he probably only had hours to live. As the Rabbi he still had to preside over the Passover meal. When that was done, they would leave the city and walk back to Bethany, the path would take them down the valley and up the other side, through the olive groves. Judas only had to tell the guards where they could ambush Jesus on the journey home.

As he spoke the blessings Jesus must have been afraid, but he had to go through with the Passover meal. He had shared many similar Seder meals with this group of family and friends, one can only guess at the emotions he felt. He had blessed the bread and wine with them many times. It's reasonable to surmise that, like anyone facing death, he wanted to be remembered. Who wouldn't? So, in his agitated state he changed the words of the blessings. He knew they would have many meals together in future without him, so he shifted the focus of his words from a re-enactment of the original Passover from Moses' time into a memorial of himself. Bear with me as I put the words into Jesus' mouth,

'This the bread of the New Covenant of the Kingdom of God. When you eat it, remember me. Like the bread becomes part of you, let me be a part of you. This the wine of the New Covenant. When you drink it, please remember me. As the wine is present, so am I present among you. Please, do this in memory of me.'

I don't think I've worded this perfectly by any means, but I think the thrust of my argument is correct. Knowing he was going to die, Jesus changed the blessing over the bread and wine, and turned it into a memorial of himself. Those listening may have been a little confused perhaps, but it was an emotional night and a great celebration. There were about five toasts in the meal and the wine was quite strong. As ever their worship will have been powerfully spiritual and uplifting. Perhaps Jesus even took some comfort from the shared religious experience.

After the meal they will have made their way out of the city, through the camps of the pilgrims in the firelight, and into the darkness on the road to Bethany.

Gethsemane

The information Judas had exchanged for his thirty pieces of silver concerned where Jesus was staying in Bethany, and thereby the route he would be taking on the way back. It was to be an ambush and, given it was dark, a potentially messy one. Each of the gospels has its own take on Jesus' capture and arrest. The basic facts are that Jesus was caught and everyone else escaped.

Which is lucky for them, because it is quite likely that any and all of his followers who had played a role in the riot in the Temple could have faced charges. But somehow only Jesus is taken into custody. I am going to pick on one detail which I think is common to all the accounts we have; Jesus gave himself up. It may be that it was the act of him giving himself up which drew the attention of the guards and allowed the others to run off into the night. There is a superb image offered in Mark's gospel. One of the guards tries to grab a fleeing disciple but grips only his cloak. The man wriggles out of it and escapes, stark naked, sprinting in terror down the hillside. It's possible an Old Testament reference actually (as ever) whereby on the day of calamity it will be like facing the enemy's army finding you forgot to get dressed that morning. But the inference is clear, it was a disastrous moment and Jesus' quick thinking saved his friends. On reflection they could even conclude that he had sacrificed himself for them...

Trials and execution

Jesus was tried by the Sanhedrin; Jerusalem's ruling council of Sadducees and Priests. The charge was blasphemy for which the punishment would be death by stoning, and they had the jurisdiction to do this. However, Jesus was not found guilty because he had not blasphemed. Many Christians would claim otherwise due to the 'Son of God' title. However, Jesus never claimed he was this. As Geza Vermes pointed out, if someone were to call him a son of God it only meant 'a good man who keeps the Law' in Jesus' time.

Jesus was then sent for a second trial before the Roman Governor, Pontius Pilate. The gospels make quite a fuss of Pilate trying to avoid sentencing Jesus to death, I doubt he would have given it a second thought. However, the Christian movement prospered in the Roman Empire, it was wise to deflect the blame for the death of your founder away from your current government! According to the gospels even the crowd (which magically appears) shouted 'crucify him'. The same crowd that Jesus inspired to riot in the Temple? That's not credible. It is self-evident that it was Pilate who applied the death penalty because crucifixion was a Roman punishment. No doubt the Sadducees and Priests in the Sanhedrin encouraged him, but the general populace shared Jesus' views and would not have cheered for his execution.

Jesus was kept overnight in the Antonine prison where the Roman guard was housed. He was probably tortured, because Roman guards were renowned for this. The crown of thorns and forty lashes are credible.

The next day he was crucified outside the city wall. Tragically his friends, disciples, and his family, including his mother, were probably there to watch. Crucifixion is a cruel way to die. Normally they left you up for a few days, there is a little seat on a crucifix so you can sit on it and ease the pain. The condemned could not resist this temptation, and it prolonged their deaths.

However, this was the Passover, the eve of the Sabbath, it would have been a poor show to have Jesus and anyone else up there noisily dying when everyone else wanted to celebrate. The gospels make this point and it's a reasonable one. So, as was the practise, a Roman guard went around the crucified men with a hammer to break their knees with a hefty blow. This ensured they could not rest on the seat, their bodies would slump down, and thus they would die of asphyxiation. It seems the guard took one look at Jesus and, to save swinging the heavy hammer, jabbed him with a spear. Jesus didn't twitch. He was already dead.

One may wonder what his last words were. I don't know, but what we can be certain of is that he did pray as death approached. Who wouldn't? According to the gospels Jesus prayed the words of Psalm 22 and, called out in seeming despair;

"My God, my God. Why have you forsaken me?"

HOW JESUS BECAME CHRIST

What I have suggested so far is, I think, reasonable but there's a massive problem now for me and my reductionist tale. It's a problem that both the Atheist and the Christian could point out. It seems absurd that the Jesus I have described above could ever have become figure he is in Christianity. My 'Jesus the nice guy from Nazareth' is too flimsy a character to bear the weight of Christian belief and expectation. How could Jesus of Nazareth become 'Jesus; God, Son and Saviour', for the whole world? Somehow one needs to trace a path of development to show how the historical person has been exponentially magnified into the Jesus Christ who has been followed by billions for 2000 years.

This path leads back into Old Testament stories and Temple rituals, as the initial group of shocked followers fought to understand the significance of the recent events. This process of understanding and interpretation began with them and continued through to the writing of the gospels, some thirty to seventy years later. They also wanted to flesh out Jesus' life story, his words and deeds. The gospel writers wrote for their local communities, not ours, they painted a Jesus for *their* readers. In a way this process continues today as Christians interpret their faith in their current context.

Blood Sacrifice

The Jews of Jesus' day believed that illness and death were punishment for sin. This is why forgiveness of sins and healing are so often linked in the gospel stories. The idea is present in the myth of 'The Fall' in Genesis, Adam and Eve are immortal until their sin (disobedience), forces their exit from paradise. This is obviously a flawed concept today since it follows that those who are healthy and wealthy must therefore by morally good. But for the disciples and family of Jesus his cruel death was shocking and needed an explanation. They must have loved him dearly. He was a good man. What sin had he committed that would deserve such a brutal execution?

Coincidentally, at the exact time of Jesus' execution another slaughter was taking place in the Temple. It may even have been audible to those stood at the foot of the cross; the bleating of innocent lambs being slain for the Passover. They were killed that afternoon in readiness for the feasts that night. The people who witnessed the death of Jesus may have made a connection between the two. The innocent Jesus, as innocent as a lamb, sacrificed. But why?

As the community pondered this mystery over the coming months and weeks, they would have quite quickly realised there was another precedent in Jewish religious life. On the feast of Yom Kippur two goats were selected. One was slaughtered on the altar and its blood was poured in the sanctuary and over the back of the remaining goat. The blood was said to represent the sins of Israel. This remaining goat, with the sins of the nation symbolically on its back, was taken to the edge of the desert and set free. It was the *scapegoat*.

The early Church conflated these two existing ideas and applied them to Jesus. He was innocent, he was sacrificed, he had no sins of his own. This gave his followers a theological theory to make sense of his death. Jesus' death was a *sacrifice*, the Lamb of God made the scapegoat for *our sins*, not his own. After all, he had *saved* the disciples from arrest in Gethsemane. With these connections made, the original disciples had a key part of the central message for a new religion in place. At this early stage however they didn't perhaps realise the revolution that was taking place in their midst. They certainly would not have predicted how much it would spread in the near future.

The Resurrection

According to Christian tradition on the Sunday after Jesus' burial some women (his mother Mary, Mary Magdalene, and his sister Salome) went to the tomb to embalm Jesus' body. When they arrived, the stone had been rolled away, and the tomb was empty. They were spoken to by an angelic figure who told them Jesus had gone ahead to Galilee. Mark's gospel ends thus;

"Terrified, the women left and ran from the tomb. They said nothing to anyone, because they were afraid..."

There are no resurrection appearances in Mark's gospel and, rather than argue the old physical versus spiritual debate I'm going to follow Mark's lead and let you make your own mind up. Whatever one makes of the resurrection of Jesus one thing is certain; his disciples, including his family, believed it was true.

Assuming they weren't all mad, or simply lying, the question needs to be asked **why** they believed Jesus had risen from the dead. There's no sensible reason to think they were insane or dishonest, or both. They had to have a genuine reason for believing Jesus was still present amongst them, because they had nothing obvious to gain from it. The question is not whether they believed *in* the resurrection, we know they did. The question is, was what did they mean *by* the resurrection?

Worship

On the Friday after Jesus' crucifixion, possibly even before, the disciples, including members of his family would have shared a meal together. Whenever it took place the occasion would be overshadowed by powerful emotions of grief, loss and déjà vu. Given the rigid format of the Seder meal there would again be a blessing of the bread and the wine before it was shared around the table. The residing rabbi would now be Jesus' brother, James.

Naturally, as he broke the bread both he and everyone present would recall the last time they did this with Jesus. They would have remembered his words at 'The Last Supper'. The blessing of the bread and wine now had a new and powerful impetus. James would have reminded them what Jesus had said and repeated his words. Instead of a simple thank you for bread and wine, the meal also became a memorial of Jesus. It had a new dimension.

Earlier I asserted that the worship of the disciples had been charismatic in nature because this seems to have been common in the early Christian Church too. Jesus' baptism by John has the hallmarks of being a charismatic religious experience (John didn't just baptise with water!) It is likely that the memorial meals shared after the death of Jesus maintained this sense of spiritual presence. Having witnessed charismatic worship myself I can honestly say it *does* feel that there is a special, holy presence in the room. The original disciples would have associated this presence with their rabbi, Jesus. When that holy presence re-occurs in their worship after Jesus death, they <u>still</u> associate it with him. Jesus is indeed among them, he is present in their worship.

Maybe the reason why Mark has no resurrection stories is that his readers didn't need them. They had 'witnessed' the presence of the risen Jesus in their worship. The resurrection appearances as they appear in the other gospels are meant to be taken as 'evidence' perhaps, but they can't really work that way, they can only be taken on faith.

It is possible that the initial belief in the resurrection of Jesus stemmed from the spiritual and <u>transcendent</u> nature of the worship of the early Church. Gospels written after Mark have stories of resurrection appearances. Jesus can walk through locked doors like a ghost, yet he is physical enough to eat some fish at a meal.

But consider the famous appearance of Jesus on the road to Emmaus;

> [30] When he was sat at the table with them, he took the bread, gave thanks, broke it and gave it to them. [31] Their eyes were opened, they

recognised him, and he disappeared from their sight. [32] They asked one another, "Did not our hearts burn within us while he talked on the road and explained the scriptures to us?"

He walks along with the two disciples, yet he is unknown and unrecognised as he teaches them. In the evening the two ask him to remain and share food with them. They recognise the 'real presence' of Jesus in the breaking of bread. This may all seem a little 'mystical' but, this is religion after all; it's where mysticism hangs out!

Pentecost

The event which marks the, in a sense re-birth, of the fledgling Christian community occurs at Pentecost. At the time the group were still probably known as preachers of the Kingdom of God message. The early Christians called themselves followers of 'The Way'. I will call this group 'Jewish Christians' because whatever they believed in; it did not separate them from the Jewish faith at this early stage. They worshipped in the synagogue and temple, they said Jewish prayers, they believed in the Kingdom of God, and they followed all the Law of Moses. The only difference was that they believed Jesus had risen from the dead, their Friday evening Seder meal had an added memorial dimension, but that wasn't breaking any of the laws of Moses.

In Luke's book of Acts, at Pentecost the central tenets of Christianity are spelled out in Peter's preaching. However, it is likely that this is written retrospectively by Luke and his Church. More importantly than what is claimed here however, is the detail that the apostles had a religious experience, again, and 'spoke in tongues'. The claim is made that everyone listening heard them in their own language, though it is not what one would normally say of the phenomenon. What would be evident would be their joy and enthusiasm. That is what bystanders understood. These people had found something, something joyful, and it was attractive to outsiders. Those witnesses, Jew and Gentile, wanted to be a part of this new, ecstatic, phenomenon.

The Split

After Jesus' death his disciples continued as before with James as the leader. Their message had changed however, they were still within Judaism, they still believed in the Kingdom of God, but, as noted above, they now had an extra element of a focus on Jesus. They believed Jesus had risen from the dead and their Friday evening Sabbath meal had become a memorial to him. The messenger had become the message and that message now contained a further new component; the prospect of a personal resurrection.

At this period in history Judaism as a religion was open to converts. There were Jewish communities across the Roman Empire and many Gentile citizens found the concept of monotheism, the belief in only one god, philosophically appealing. The Graeco-Roman religious model with lots of gods quarrelling etc. lacked intellectual rigour and was a little silly. The moral code inspired by the Holy texts of Judaism was also admired. Many Gentiles became *proselytes* and enjoyed a kind of adopted Jewish status. When these people heard about a new religious movement following Jesus, it began to attract potential members.

This split the original 'Christian' group in two; those who welcomed the Gentile converts (The Hellenist Christians, from the Greek word for Greece - Hellas) and those who did not (The Jewish Christians). The Jewish group were made up of Jesus' original followers led by James. The Hellenists looked up to the original, founding group as having authority, and they did not have their own leader at first, but one soon emerged.

The Hellenist Christian movement began to spread in the Jewish diaspora across the Empire, but back in Judea they had a problem. When they had their Sabbath, Seder, meal they invited Gentiles along. Their reasoning was that the meaning of the meal had changed, it was now a memorial dedicated to Jesus, it wasn't really a Jewish thing. However Jewish law stated that eating with Gentiles was a sin and if someone did it repeatedly, then they could face the death penalty. Gentiles made the food ritually unclean. The Sanhedrin appointed an enthusiastic Pharisee named Saul to root and out and arrest the offenders.

However, whilst journeying to Damascus to arrest these *Jewish* law breakers Saul had a religious experience. One could say a lot about this, it is one of the most important episodes in history, but its outcome was that Saul became a Christian convert. He wanted to join the Christian Church in Judea, but they would not accept him, as he had recently been arresting their members. He was forced to join the Hellenist Christians outside Judea. To prove his commitment to the Hellenist cause, he changed his name from Saul to its Greek version; Paul.

He was very successful expanding the movement and founding new church communities. There had initially been a major obstacle to this expansion. To join Christianity, new converts had to learn about the faith, get baptised and be circumcised. The problem is obvious. Circumcision, without any anaesthetic, for an adult male was painful and dangerous. So, Paul dropped the requirement and to further ease the process he also abandoned the rule that Christians had to abstain from pork.

These two steps enabled Paul's missionary work, but they scandalised the founding Christian group which included the original disciples and Jesus' family. In Galatians chapters 1 and 2 the conflict is laid bare. Paul is opposed to James. Peter is uncertain of what to do, and is afraid of James. In Acts chapter 15 a compromise agreement appears to have been put in place, but this looks like later Christian editing of events. I suspect the two groups simply agreed to disagree. Twenty years after Jesus' death there were effectively two Christian churches; a Jewish one and a Gentile one.

Inevitably the time came when the original disciples began to die out and there was a need to write down the Church's teaching about Jesus. It was a body of teaching that was actually growing. You might expect the opposite, that the number of anecdotes about Jesus would decrease as people forgot them, far from it. Christian preachers were developing the original ideas, making them fit in new environments and making them address new problems. Luke had some excellent new parables; The Good Samaritan and The Prodigal Son to name two.

James probably died around 62 CE. According to Josephus he was thrown off the top of the Temple walls and stoned to death to finish him off. He was a popular figure and had a reputation for holiness, prayer, and faithfulness to the Torah. His murder probably angered many people, he was also the brother of Jesus and leader of the first Church, you might ask 'how come he's so unknown'?

The answer lies in the fact that the gospels were written by a Gentile Church inspired by Paul. James' very Jewish Christianity was an embarrassment to them. The gospels play down the Jewishness of Jesus, his family and his first followers. James was certainly one of the original disciples however, when you look at the so-called lists of the apostles there's a plethora of James'. By multiplying the number of James', the writers deliberately confuse the reader (as Robert Eisenman points out). All the gospels in the New Testament preach the Gentile, Greek Christianity of Paul and his followers. They're no fan of James because he's too Jewish for their tastes.

Shortly after James death, and maybe linked to it, Judea rose up in rebellion against Rome. The rebellion was crushed, the Temple in Jerusalem was flattened except for the Western Wall. Thousands were killed or taken as slaves. By 70CE the only remaining Jewish movement from Jesus' time were the Pharisees. Given the destruction of the Temple, all the central feasts of Judaism needed re-shaping. Judaism became a religion of the book and the synagogue. At the Council of Jamnia (records on this are scant) it seems the Pharisees decided to boot out the 'Jewish Christians' since they were saying some odd things about Jesus. Judaism was being renewed minus its Temple, they had to focus on what they believed, and the followers of Jesus weren't kosher enough.

It may be that the group led by James had left Jerusalem shortly after his death. Records are fragmentary but it is possible that they later became known as the Ebionite Church. They were excommunicated for heresy by mainstream Christianity for rejecting the idea that Jesus was the Son of God. Alas the evidence is too slim to be confident of this judgement.

Unlike its Jewish counterpart, the Hellenist church was spreading very effectively making many new converts. Its message of an afterlife in heaven in exchange for faith in Jesus was very popular with women and slaves across the Empire. The original teachings of Jesus lost their moorings in their Jewish context. The notion of the Kingdom of God being about the freeing of Israel from Roman dominion became irrelevant. The Kingdom of God came to mean the Church, or paradise, or resurrection into God's heavenly Kingdom. It was flexible. The Church now had a message of personal salvation with Jesus as your Saviour.

There were stories that referred to Jesus as the son of god, in the Roman Empire Caesar was considered divine so how could Jesus, the Messiah for all mankind, be anything less? Gentile Christians promoted Jesus to the status of The Son of God. The Jesus church prayed to Yahweh/God, but the new Gentile Christians worshipped Jesus, so he had to become divine. A few hundred years later this understanding is formalised (fossilised?) in the Nicene Creed.

CONCLUSION?

In the first half of this book the picture of Jesus as preacher, teacher, healer, exorcist is, I think, faithful to the historical person of Jesus. In the second half I tried to show how the circumstances of his death, and the effect of that on his disciples, shaped their understanding of the meaning and *significance* of those events. Crucial to the new image of Jesus that emerges is the use of the Old Testament to explain Jesus' life. Between 33 and 64 CE, whenever they saw a gap, the Christian missionaries developed their teachings using Old Testament stories. This is very evident in the Birth narratives and, indeed, whenever eyewitness testimony is unavailable or scant.

There was a Jesus of history, but the Church that wrote the Gospels presents a Jesus Christ who is the focus of their faith. Matthew, Mark, Luke and John were not biographers, they were theologians. The life and death of Jesus of Nazareth is the inspiration for the Gospels, he's still visible in there, but they have transformed him into the focus of a religion. As I stated earlier, the messenger became the message.

Most people have their own views on Jesus, Christianity, and God and this book may have either informed or irritated you. It is valid to ponder how much of what I have said is likely to be true. It is certainly true to say that when the evidence is slim, the conclusions can only be tentative.

You can believe that all the New Testament is historical fact if you want to, but I'd say believe it for what it is. Parts of it are historical, parts are exaggerated or developed, parts are mythical. That is the nature of the gospel genre but that doesn't undermine the *value* of the gospels. Myths offer great insight into life's trials, joys and mysteries. The validity of a myth isn't to be found in the question 'did it actually happen?', rather it is in the question 'is this myth useful to us?' The measure of a myth is utility not historicity.

For example, consider the widely ridiculed myth of the six-day creation story in Genesis. Many like to point out that this is contradicted by the theories of the Big Bang and Evolution. That's akin to saying 'Finding Nemo' is contradicted by marine biology. One can only compare like with like. The Genesis creation story(ies) offers neither science nor history.

If, like the fundamentalist Christians you think the earth was created in six days then you're simply ignoring reality. Scientific questions can only be answered by science. Science is excellent at that, but it is not very useful when seeking for meaning and worth in the universe. It can tell us how to build an atomic bomb, morality (religious and otherwise) is our guide as to whether we should use it.

Religion does not have a monopoly on morality, it does have brilliant insights to offer. Of course, religious people should remember that religions have made evil moral decisions in the past and in the present. Just because a moral principle is enshrined in a religious text doesn't mean it is automatically 'good'; it needs to be tested against human experience. For example, teachings from the book of Leviticus whereby homosexuality is condemned can be happily slung in the bin. Just because an ancient tribe thought homosexuality was sinful doesn't mean we have to. It's just silly to believe ancient prejudices are divine teaching.

Was the resurrection, physical or spiritual? It doesn't matter, if you believe Jesus has risen it needs to be something you have *experienced*, not read about. If you are a Christian, then the nature of his 'presence' in the Upper Room at Pentecost isn't important, what is important is that he is present in your life.

I genuinely believe Christianity is a valid and worthwhile religion to follow. However, I can't personally abandon the distinction between myth and reality. Religion has to be justifiable in rational terms and Christianity has to have its roots in actual events. Mysticism, spirituality, transcendence, call it what you will, has its place. It's a narrow view of life that would exclude them. I can't find the meaning of life in science and I think it's a ludicrous demand to place on that field of study.

The Jesus who lived in his time was real enough. The Christ of the gospels is based on him but is wrapped up in theological myths to make sense of the questions of existence, birth, life and death. If the gospel myths work for you that is good, myths are true enough in their appropriate mythical context. But there's no need to throw away your reason and believe in a magical Disney Jesus, walking on water. It would be a great magic trick, but it suggests he couldn't swim.

Faced with its decline in the present, too much of Christianity is retreating into the safety of the past. There are too many Evangelicals hiding behind the Bible, too many Catholics hiding behind tradition. Which is ironic, since Christianity's strength historically was an ability to speak to the present, to adapt its traditions.

Jesus' 'Golden Rule' demands that his followers engage practically with the present, in the real world, and care for our neighbour. That's no bad thing.

FURTHER READING:

For the record I studied the New Testament under Doctor John McGuckin who later became Professor McGuckin at Union Theological Seminary, New York. He inspired me a great deal, especially with his superb exegesis (analysis) of Mark's gospel. I don't have a clue if he would agree with what I've written here and I'm not claiming to be representing his ideas.

Some books I would like to mention for varying reasons are;
- 'An Introduction to the New Testament' by Raymond Brown.
- 'Jesus the Jew' by Geza Vermes.
- 'James the Brother of Jesus' by Robert Eisenman.
- If you'd like to look up the authentic words of Jesus, I recommend you Google 'The Jesus Seminar' a part of the Westar Institute, they are valid, serious scholars.

I hope you are more cautious when reading scripture having read this little book. The Bible is full of pitfalls for the unwary. Don't read an antiquated translation like the King James version. Just because it sounds like Shakespeare doesn't make it literature. For the purposes of my arguments here you could check out the following.
- The gospel of Mark. Remember that the original ended at chapter 16 verse 8 and there are no resurrection stories in it. He names Jesus' brothers in chapter 6 verse 3.
- St Paul's letter to the Galatians chapters 1 and 2. The controversy and conflict between Paul's Gentile Christianity and James Jewish version are self-evident. Paul is sarcastic about James and castigates Peter for his cowardice.
- Acts chapter 15. In the Jerusalem meeting the conflict is 'solved' supposedly. Look who leads the meeting and who announces the compromise, it's James, not Peter.
- Psalm 22, from which Jesus called out in seeming despair; "My God, my God. Why have you forsaken me?' The Psalm isn't long, it starts off in despair but when you get to the last section it reads like a prophecy for a

new world religion. Substitute the word 'Lord' for 'Jesus' and see what happens. I think that's what the early Christians did.

ENDNOTE; WHY I AM NOT AN ATHEIST

After some discussion I have decided to include this section, though I had originally deleted it. Since I have claimed to believe in a God, it seems reasonable that I should explain why. The answer to that is quite personal and the tone of this section is different to the rest of this book. Basically, I think there are two reasons why I believe in a God. Actually, there's probably more, but I haven't worked them out.

First Reason: My Religious Experience.

In March 1982 I decided I needed to attend a religious retreat to sort my life out and reflect on my faith. So, one day in July I boarded the train at Manchester Piccadilly Station and set off down south.

I was 22 and, with regard to my potential talents my life had yet to start. In fact, my potential talents were a mystery. I had failed to access my escape route out of British Telecommunications into a career as an actor. My life felt like a trap; I could not change my circumstances.

St Cassian's Centre, Kintbury, is residential retreat centre for young people. It is set in the lush (compared to North Manchester) Berkshire countryside, surrounded by farms. It takes retreatants mainly from the sixth forms of Catholic schools and colleges. The centre was founded on the vision of Brother Damian Lundy (and others) to meet the peculiar needs of the age group.

I was put in a small discussion/prayer group led by Brother Celestine who was a cuddly bear of an Irish monk in his late fifties. I felt those first few days were a liberation for me, and I loved it. Maybe because people a little younger than me were listening to what I had to say, they didn't think I was stupid. I was able to give to them and help them. People cared enough to listen to me. I felt valued as a person. It's not that this had never happened before, but it happened with such force during the first half of that week.

By the Wednesday I was rejuvenated, I had learned as much as I could and was ready to return home. A little deflated, since I still didn't know where I was going in life, but I had a new sense of self-belief that would surely help me. All these young people, many of whom were getting ready for university, had surrounded me. A myriad of careers and opportunities lay at their feet. For me it was back to Oldham telephone exchange and routine electrical maintenance. There was a danger that a door had opened onto a brighter world but that this would prove an inaccessible mirage.

The Wednesday morning found me stood in the car park, waiting to weed the brother's potato patch. Celestine seemed to have read my thoughts on the progress of the week so far. He came over to me as I waited in my hat and gloves looking forward to a bit of manual labour. He wished me good morning and asked how I was. The conversation went something like this:

"John, have you enjoyed the week so far? Do you feel you have got a lot out of it?

"Yes. It has been great." I replied. Yes, it had been great, but I was realising that for me nothing had really changed, and I was ready to go home.

"You think the weeks' over don't you, John? You think there's nothing else to come."

Ooh! I had been rumbled! I muttered some kind of agreement. How did he know this was how I felt? Celestine was certainly a man who thought more than he said. He continued;

"John, I have been asked to pray with you, would you like to do that?" He asked.

"Well, err... thanks very much Celestine, I'll pray for you too." 'What a nice man.' I thought.

"No, that's not what I mean." He continued. "You need to be there; I have been told to pray with you."

"Who by?" I asked.

"Well, I have a kind of hot line to the Holy Spirit. The phone rang, and I was told to pray with you. It's something you need John."

Several thoughts went through my mind. Firstly, he was barmy. Secondly, I had a good deal of respect already for Celestine, and I knew it was nothing scary or cultish. Thirdly, it sounded it embarrassing, a little weird and rather pointless. Fourthly, was anyone else getting this special offer? I asked him and he said no. He'd only been asked to pray with me. Period. That was the clincher; I'd paid £10 more than the students, a whole £76, so I was pleased to be getting a little extra for my cash. I was getting a bargain. 'Count me in' I thought.

"Of course, Celestine, I'd be very happy for you to pray with me. Shall I bring my guitar?" I could knock out a quick hymn I reasoned.

"No. Just bring yourself."

I think by then he had realised that he was dealing the spiritually illiterate, and he arranged the time and place to meet me the next day. The next 24 hours passed uneventfully. On the Thursday afternoon I headed up to the 'Winchester room' to meet Celestine so he could pray for me.

I was a little disappointed on arrival as I saw that Richard, one of the team, was there. I liked the guy, but he was younger than me and this somehow watered down the special attention I was to get. I also had one eye on the clock. I had arranged to practise a song for the last night concert with a girl who, quite coincidentally you understand, was very attractive. I rather hoped this prayer thing would be over fairly sharpish. It simply was something I would add to my diary; *'God told Celestine to pray with me (and no one else, ha ha). He did, and it was very nice.'* End of diary entry.

There I was in the room with the two of them. Celestine told me what I had to do once the greetings were over and done.

"Just sit there, John. Richard and I will begin by praying for you. All you need do is try to be open to the Holy Spirit.

They sat either side of me and took one of my hands each. This touching other men stuff was something I wasn't very comfortable with but had got a little more used to it at Kintbury. It was OK to hold Celestine's hand, Richard, I decided, had better watch who he told about the arrangement. They began to pray for me, thanking God for the wonderful young person that I was. Having nothing to do I chipped in with a few 'Our Fathers' of my own and was just embarking on a 'Glory be' when Celestine stopped me.

"No John. You don't need to do anything. We'll pray for you. You just try to be open to the Holy Spirit."

So, I shut up, and they carried on. I didn't know what to do; but I didn't know how to do nothing. Feeling rather futile, I followed instructions to the letter and repeated the word 'open' in my mind. This was now embarrassing, and I felt somewhat ashamed. I felt useless because I did not know what to do. How apt, these feelings were my life in microcosm. I was lost on the journey of my life and could not help myself. My sense of my own worthlessness came back too, thanks guys! Surrounded by these young people with prospects all week had underlined how hopeless my position was. I was quite upset, and a few tears began to flow. This had only taken five minutes. Richard remarked on the fact as the two of them stopped praying.

"That was quick Celestine, he must be really ready for this."

I was not too pleased. I was already aware of how I felt about my life and I didn't really see a need to thank either of them for reminding me and bringing it all out so emotionally. Had I known this prayer thing would merely upset me I would not have come along. I got up to leave; I was heading for the door as Celestine stopped me.

"No John, that's not it, that's just the start."

I was not enjoying the proceedings, and I was in a rush to get my guitar and practise the song with the very attractive girl. It was a thought which cheered me a little, I was bound to get her phone number at least. Reluctantly, I turned back into the room hoping it would be over soon and I could go. I think Celestine was aware of how unhappy I felt. Then again, that is why I was in the room in the first place; it was bound to be 'difficult' at some point. Looking back, it must have been touch and go whether or not I just turned and walked out. If I stayed it was only because I trusted Celestine.

The two of them removed a long coffee table from the centre of the room and asked me to stand with my back to the gap on the carpet that they had created. They stood either side of me, holding my arms, clearly ready to lower me into the space. I was a little upset still and not feeling particularly cooperative. I was only prepared to go through the motions, whatever they were to be, so as not to hurt Celestine's feelings.

"OK John, just relax, don't fight whatever happens, and don't be afraid."

With the last bit of good will that remained in me I tried to comply. Instantly I felt myself swooning into a faint, my knees buckled. It was as if someone had given me a powerful anaesthetic, and it was scary. 'Whoa', I thought, 'No thank you' and I stood bolt upright.

"John, relax. Do not be afraid."

But I was afraid. I had nearly keeled over in a faint, bollocks to not being afraid! In that moment, strangely, I understood that I had missed an opportunity. I did not know what that opportunity had been. Whatever it was, however, I cannot trust anyone that much. I would not, could not, let go of my self-control. Not for anyone. The situation turned to farce. Celestine and Richard pushed back on my shoulders, I pushed forward tensing the muscles in my upper body. It was like rugby training for the front row of the scrum.

I was aware that this was, again, becoming an embarrassment. I reasoned that the only way out was to go along with the charade. I feigned unconsciousness and let them drop me to the floor. I banged my head slightly as they laid me down, Richard noted it, but Celestine reckoned I was OK. I lay there keeping my eyes closed, they both prayed for me, again thanking God for the person I was, thanking God for the things I had done for others that week. I was in a better mood by now. I was in control as long as I played my part and let them get on with the holy compliments. I prepared to wait it out.

Five or ten minutes passed in this manner. As I lay there, it crossed my mind that I would have to tell my mates what had happened at Kintbury. They thought I was a nutcase simply for going on the retreat. I imagined the conversation in the pub.

'So, John, what did you get up to on the retreat thing then?'

'Err, I went into this room and I laid on the floor with these two blokes.'

Their response to that didn't bear thinking about. I felt myself beginning to snigger as I lay on the carpet listening to their prayers. After a struggle I regained my composure. I pinched the flesh on the back of my thighs quite hard (an act which must have been visible) and this stopped me giggling. After a short while I was back in control and I decided that, after all, they were trying to do me a favour. I reciprocated this by praying for both of them. As I lay there, an image of the cross did come through to me. It was from my bedroom at home. A cross created by the shadow of the window frame in my bedroom through the closed curtains. It is a cross I'd seen all my life. I thought about this image and felt let down by its banality, although it is a touching memory for me now.

It became a gently meditative/dull half hour or so as I waited for the two of them to stop waffling on. If I'd been really 'out' of course I would not have known how long I had been lay there. What strikes me is that I did not really give myself up to the experience. For half of the time I was consciously trying not to laugh, which does not suggest a profound spiritual trip to me. For the other half of the time I was trying to fill a boring lie down with some prayers and general daydreaming. I am certain I was in full control for all but one split second, but then I had stepped back from the brink of giving myself over.

I'd decided to let them finish, give it a couple of minutes and then get up exclaiming what a wacky experience it had all been. 'Thanks guys, hey, you can really do your prayer stuff, wow, praise the Lord, etc.' In the event, sensing they weren't nearby, I opened one eye and had a surreptitious peep around the room. Nobody watching, good. Next, I produced my 'Hey, I'm coming out of a trance act'.

I got to my feet, thanked them in a suitable manner, and headed for the door. Celestine stopped me suggesting that I might need to take a breather. I assured him I felt fine. However, I sat down and found myself facing some kind of expectation from them that they might see the results of their, and the Holy Spirit's, handiwork. Of course, I had little to relate, and they knew the kind of things I should have said. From experience they knew the state I should have been in. Celestine read the smirk that was growing on my face with each lie I was telling. I'd been taking the piss, and he knew. He paused and thought a while. I wonder what went through his mind? He must have asked himself if he had he misheard the message on the hot line. Perhaps the message from the Holy Spirit had included the word 'not' and he'd misheard it. In the event I think he trusted to his spiritual discernment and experience.

"OK John." He smiled. "Are you off to play this song of yours now?"

"Yes." I replied. "I'm a little late."

"Fine. Would you do something for me? Before you go to your rehearsal, go for a short walk, you'll feel much better. After that you'll feel very tired and you'll need to go for a rest."

"Course I will Celestine." I responded, and, relieved to escape, left the room.

Walking down the corridor, under the eaves of the old building, I felt a certain lightness of mood that I was now free to see this girl. I also had a nagging thought that I'd let Celestine down. I reasoned that it wasn't my fault he was a loony. Yet, somewhere in the last hour or so I felt I had been a fraud, I shouldn't have played along with it. I decided I'd do as he requested. There was no really significant reason why, and no expectation on my part.

I only committed to a short stroll, just across the car park, and onto the main drive out of St Cassian's between the fields. It was a lovely, sunny, summer's day and in the setting of the Berkshire countryside a walk is no chore. After that I would walk back round the house, to the wing where I was staying, and get my guitar. It would not take long and, anyway, I would have to apologise for being late as it was. Nothing lost then. I went downstairs and ambled across the gravel yard at the front of the house. There was no one around. It was a peaceful, mellow afternoon, and I headed out past the trees and just outside the gates of St. Cassian's.

It is a beautiful place, and I was able to appreciate that having been brought up in suburban Manchester. As I walked beyond the gates, I turned to look at some cows grazing in a field, a serene scene on a sunny day. The horizon was a line of trees behind the field. 'It's beautiful'. With a smile on my face I said that phrase in my mind a couple of times. Then I said it aloud, looking at the cows, the field, the trees.

"It's beautiful."

My smile grew as I began to feel a sense of joy and peace and happiness. I also laughed a little.

"It's beautiful!"

I said again, louder. It was beautiful, such beauty. I had to say it aloud.

"It's beautiful, it's beautiful, it's beautiful."

I began to shout at the scene before my eyes.

"BEAUTIFUL!"

As I shouted, my voice turned to a drunken bellow. I was literally intoxicated with the beauty of it. My jaw was hanging slackly and my arms wide open to embrace what I saw, staggering in the road like a drunk. Emotionally I felt a wave or surge of love come from the ground and up through my feet, it seemed to burst through the top of my head, as if I were a firework, and shoot up into the sky. It was a force outside of me, but it filled me, I resonated as though I were a string on a musical instrument heavily drawn by a bow. I was in tune with a force that was always there if we could but find its pitch.

My soul sang. Sobbing, I roared with joy as I stared at the line of trees. It was as though the sun was setting behind them, and then it changed its mind and started to come through the trees towards me. And I saw that the field, the cows, the trees, the fabric of the world was insubstantial compared to this light. I stood; arms outstretched facing it. The light was not blinding, it understated its power. It was a vision of the emotional explosion I was feeling. I put a name to it, and I realised that it was a feeling of being loved.

Once I had named the word; love, once I had understood that much, I was aware of taking an objective view. From then on, the vision began to fade. My heart rate started to return to normal, and I took some deep breaths. I knew there was more to be seen, more to be felt, but that my vision was limited by my capacity to appreciate it. I felt it was infinite, and I had seen as much as I could take and remain sane.

The more my process of rationalising what had happened 'kicked in' the further the visionary state receded. Finally, I was stood, crouching, with my mouth wide open, my arms outstretched, but sagging. I had dribbled saliva onto my chin and shirt. Now that I was aware of this last fact a thought struck me, 'What if someone had seen me?' I wasn't ready to explain myself and it was a potentially embarrassing scene. I pulled myself upright and regained my composure as best I could.

I looked back at the view and it had returned to normal. The cows grazed, the sun shone, the trees graced the horizon as beautifully as before. I was confused, but I knew then that something extraordinary had happened. I knew also that I would spend a long time trying to understand it all. I still probe the event for meaning even now. I knew it *meant* something back then, but I did not know what. I knew that I had to put off thinking about it. In retrospect, perhaps, I should have gone back to Celestine and shared it with him. In fact, later when I tried to speak to him, I failed to connect properly, I don't know why. He didn't seem interested. As I decided to delay any reflection, I remembered I had a rehearsal to play for, though that seemed less important now. I decided I would make my way back to the De La Salle wing of the house to get my guitar.

I walked back down the lane to the car park. There was a gate at the side, that led to a path that led under the massive cedar tree at the side of the house. I recollected Celestine saying I would feel tired and would need a rest. 'What a strange fellow' I thought. I felt fine. As I raised my foot to climb a step near the old orchard, did I feel a little fatigued, perhaps? Maybe. I decided not to go for the next step up but to bring my feet together on the first step. No need to rush then. For the next step I grasped my right thigh with both my hands and dragged this leaden limb up to step number two, thankfully the final stage of my ascent. I dragged my left leg up by using my body weight and stumbled forward, propelled gravity. I staggered forward like a drunk looking for somewhere to vomit. The rest of the journey I spent weaving, half bent over, falling over, and bouncing off trees in the orchard in an approximation of my intended direction. Eventually I got to the downstairs outside door of the De La Salle wing. All the time I groaned in exhaustion,

"I'm knackered, oh, I'm so tired, oh God, I'm shattered."

At the door I leaned on the handle and thankfully it opened inwards. I stumbled against it and collapsed in a heap inside the hall. Some people were inside and saw me slump to the floor. At first, they laughed and suggested I had visited the 'Blue Ball' pub in Kintbury. As I tottered to my feet, they became concerned and enquired after my health. I was climbing the stairs on my knees trying to drag myself up with my hands clutching the banister rail.

"Are you sure you're OK John?"

"I'm knackered," I grunted, "Just want to get to my room. Lie down. I'm knackered."

I wasn't very civil to them. I think they recognised this as being out of character and they came to my help. Two of them picked me up and heaved me upstairs. With their assistance I lurched through the door of my room and flopped backwards onto the bed.

I guess they ran to get one of the De la Salle brothers to make sure I was not ill, because I remember Damian, came to check on me.

"Are you OK John? Have you been down to the pub?" He asked.

"No. Celestine. Celestine... He said some prayers." I grunted. With that Damian's tone utterly changed.

"Oh, that's OK. You just rest as much as you need to." He seen this before!

A few other heads poked around the door and asked if I was OK. I was not functioning properly, but I dimly remember that I tried to reassure them. I may have been a little abrupt. I seemed drained of all energy. I didn't fall asleep for a while, but I cannot be certain. It was dark when I got up later that evening; given it was summer that must have been at least 9.30 pm.

As I lay there, I reflected a little on what had happened. I felt an urge to say, 'thank you', as if it was a simple prayer. I let the faces of anyone I had ever known, family, friends, work mates, teachers, and people at Kintbury drift into my mind's eye. As they appeared, I thanked God for the gifts they had been to me. I thanked God for the people I loved, for the people I hated and for those in between. It was a very peaceful experience for me to do this. Then I nodded off. When I finally arose, late that evening, I was rested if not back up to full strength.

The thing about co called 'religious experiences' is that they are meaningless unless they are linked to a tangible change in the person. Spiritual fireworks on their own make for an empty display. That idea did not occur to me at the time, I had no clear thoughts on the matter back then.

The next day we went on a trip to Brighton by coach. It was a day out of the retreat, for sunbathing, and a couple of beers on the seafront. On the return journey Brother Damian sat next to me and we had our chat about why I had come to Kintbury and where my life was going. I told him about my failed attempts to get into drama school and become an actor. He was a good listener which was nice. Voicing his thoughts, he noted how well I got on with the other retreatants; I certainly did not lack personal and social skills.

"John, have you ever considered becoming a teacher? He asked.

"Er... no. I can't. I'm thick." I laughed.

"How do you know you are thick?"

"I didn't do well at school, I couldn't do it. I've only got four O levels, all grade C's You have to go to university and things like that if you want to be a teacher."

"Did you like school?"

"No, I hated it."

"Why?"

"I couldn't see the point of it."

"Well, that doesn't mean you're thick. Maybe if you did see the point of it, you might be good at it."

"What would be the point of that?" I asked.

"You could go to university, study to become a teacher. You would make a good teacher."

"How do you know?"

"I can tell."

"Oh."

"Why don't you have a think about it? Think about becoming a teacher."

"OK."

I sat quietly looking out of the window. After a couple of minutes, I turned back to Damian.

"A teacher? OK then. I'll do that." I said.

"What? What do you mean?"

"I'm going to be a teacher. It was your idea."

"Yes, but you have to think about it John."

"I just have."

"But, I meant for longer than that. Take a few weeks, or months. Take a year."

"I don't need to. I've just thought about it and that's what I'm going to do."

Damian was understandably taken aback by the speed of my decision. To anyone listening my response must have appeared superficial as I did not appear to have reflected sensibly on his idea. From my perspective, however, as soon as he had made the suggestion 'the lights came on'.

My life changed over the course of the next six years. I passed my maths O level at night school. A year later, aided by a good deal of luck I scraped an A level in Sociology also at night school. I was more successful at General Studies A level getting a grade C, despite going for a pint between the two papers on the day! I went to college in Southampton got a 2:1 in Theology coming top of my course, and an immense source of pride to myself and my parents, I studied to be a teacher at Cambridge University.

Naturally (perhaps) this series of events sways me even today towards theism. They make up the fulcrum on which my life pivoted and on which it, and I, changed. The only question for me about the experience is 'was I hypnotised?'

Well, as a qualified hypnotherapist myself I can see the similarities; there was an induction (relax) and a post hypnotic suggestion (go for a walk, something will happen). Having undergone hypnosis many times in my training, I know what it feels like as the subject, and I know what to look for as the hypnotherapist. You cannot hypnotise people unless they agree to it, so the induction didn't work, I had resisted it. The post hypnotic suggestion was too vague to be effective. Celestine did not outline what I was meant to experience, so he was not its author.

Second Reason: The First Cause Argument.

The 'First Cause' or 'Cosmological' argument is a philosophical construct. It does not prove that a Creator (1st Cause) exists because that is impossible. In fairness to Plato, who first stated the argument, he didn't believe it worked either, though he wasn't a theist in any modern sense of that word. The argument runs thus:

Premise 1   Individual events have a cause.
Premise 2   The totality of events (the universe) has a 1st cause.
Conclusion   That 1st cause is what a theist would call God.

There are a number of logical reasons why the argument cannot prove a Creator God. One is that the conclusion, an uncaused cause, is utterly different from the argument preceding it where everything has a cause. Additionally, the conclusion raises the inevitable question 'what caused the 1st Cause'? So it fails. The First Cause Argument does not prove a Creator God but, allied with our knowledge of science, we may point out that the 'cause' of the universe is the Big Bang. But, what caused that?

I think there are only three possible answers to this question and *none* of them can be proven:

1. The universe is eternal, a series of 'Big Bangs' and 'Big Crunches' and has no cause.
2. The Universe has no cause, the question is meaningless since there is nothing before the 'Big Bang'. The universe 'just is'.
3. The 'Big Bang' was initiated by a Creator God.

The infinite series of 'Big Bangs' and 'Big Crunches' doesn't answer the question since, if it were true, then it too would require an explanation. It's an alternative version of the second one that follows, that the universe 'just is'. That's a valid response to the question, but it's not a very satisfying answer. As far as I can see it's no better than the Creator God answer, in fact, it's worse. Anyway, neither can be proven.

It would seem that belief in a Creator God is down to faith or, how one makes sense of existence. A lot of things in life cannot be scientifically proven. We use concepts like 'love', 'beauty', 'justice', 'good' and 'bad' every day. They are very important to us, but they cannot be empirically proven because they are not things. We have to accept them on 'faith', or on 'life experience'.

I can be charged with diminishing the nature of God here, for reducing the creator to a 'reasonable idea'. However, I'm not saying that is merely what God *is*, but it is all I can reasonably argue for. In my head there is more to the being I call 'God' than is present in my arguments, but it is a matter of faith, not science or logic. I don't think there's anything wrong with that.

www.ingramcontent.com/pod-product-compliance
Lightning Source LLC
Chambersburg PA
CBHW020443030426

42337CB00014B/1374